T0195062

Endorsements

This book's approach or premise is something relatable. It talks about people in general—our faith, hope. And in times of adversities, how we experience and handle frustrations, temptations, negativities, fears, uncertainties, low self-esteem, and insecurities in our circumstances and situations that prevent us from achieving our hearts' desires.

There are so many essential aspects of the book that I can delve on. Every page reflects how God sees us and how he can solve our problems. Her stories' humor was a pleasant surprise.

The book is inspiring, fulfilling, and reassuring. It's a perfect book.

—Alicia Saccoccia, dedicated mother of two Autistic children, loving wife, and former Blue Cross Blue Shield Associate.

Wow! Words do have power, and yours are timely.

I love your book. What a wonderful commentary about life in general and about the times we live in. Addressing insecurities and lack of confidence in the young and adding in your life journey make this book so relatable.

Philippians 4:8 is one of my favorite passages. So good. You tell folks how to pray. Charlotte's poem is a great bonus. I smiled, and I rejoiced in your words. I cannot wait for the finished book to be in my hands.

So proud of you! Thank you for allowing me to get a sneak peek.

—Bette Brownlee, Library Media Tech in the Cajon Valley Union School District, El Cajon, CA. Schools listed as Madison and Rancho San Diego Elementary Schools.

Through God's Eyes is a good read! It inspires and encourages us to see ourselves as God sees us. God has a plan for our lives; he has given us all a purpose in life.

In this book, Avis shares some real-life issues and how she often felt like she did not matter. She could not see the greatness that God placed in her. After seeking the Lord and reading his Word, she was transformed and began to see herself through God's eyes!

The Lord has a plan for our lives, and his methods are more significant than the ideas we have for ourselves. This book is filled with life experiences that anyone can relate to; it also has terrific scripture references. If you are feeling unimportant, unvalued, isolated, and alone, this book is for you!

—Phyllis Wooley, Office Manager for Wooley Appraisals, Stone Mountain, Ga. A member of Free Chapel at the Gwinnett Campus in Atlanta GA. and serves as a greeter.

Previous Work

Girls … God's Best 4 U

*   *   *

Other Works

A Christmas to Remember (Play)
The Whole Armor of God (Puppetry Skit)
Somewhere Over the Rainbow (Puppetry Skit)
The Alabaster Box (Play)
A Voice from the Past (Play)

THROUGH GOD'S EYES

AVIS D. BROWNLEE-WOOLEY

WESTBOW
PRESS®
A DIVISION OF THOMAS NELSON
& ZONDERVAN

WestBow Press books may be ordered through booksellers or by contacting:

WestBow Press
A Division of Thomas Nelson & Zondervan
1663 Liberty Drive
Bloomington, IN 47403
www.westbowpress.com
844-714-3454

Interior Image Credit: Naomi Aniya Brisker

Scripture taken from the King James Version of the Bible.

Scripture quotations marked (GNT) are from the Good News Translation in Today's English Version- Second Edition Copyright © 1992 by American Bible Society. Used by Permission.

Scripture taken from the Amplified Bible, Copyright © 1954, 1958, 1962, 1964, 1965, 1987 by The Lockman Foundation. Used with permission.

Scripture quotations taken from The Holy Bible, New International Version® NIV® Copyright © 1973 1978 1984 2011 by Biblica, Inc. TM. Used by permission. All rights reserved worldwide.

ISBN: 978-1-6642-1607-5 (sc)
ISBN: 978-1-6642-1606-8 (hc)
ISBN: 978-1-6642-1608-2 (e)

Library of Congress Control Number: 2020924582

Print information available on the last page.

WestBow Press rev. date: 01/07/2021

DEDICATED TO

To all blood-washed believers who want to experience more of God's presence in their daily walk. To you I dedicate this book for your edification so that you may stand amid difficult times and remain courageous and strong.

> And he gave some, apostles, and some, prophets; and some evangelist; and some pastors and teachers; For the perfecting of the saints, for the work of the ministry, for the edifying of the body of Christ: Till we all come in the unity of the faith and of the knowledge of the Son of God, unto a perfect man, unto the measure of the status of the fulness of Christ. Ephesians 4:11–13 KJV

CONTENTS

FOREWORD

Once again, my friend Avis has drawn on the rich experience of a life lived in harmony with the Holy Spirit to weave a rich tapestry of encouragement for today's believers and nonbelievers alike. Scriptures and passages from the Bible are combined with life experiences to reinforce the hopes of all believers, regardless of age or level of spiritual maturity.

In difficult times, it's reassuring to have a godly message to encourage us to remember whose children we are and where we're going. From cover to cover, Avis reminds the reader of our importance to God and his desire to care for, nurture, and protect us.

Sandra D. North, MT(ASCP), Graduate of Self Memorial Hospital School of Medical Technology, Greenwood, South Carolina; Member of Fellowship Bible Church, Roswell, Georgia. Most importantly a woman of faith.

PREFACE

Since publishing my last book and writing other materials, I felt the urge in my spirit to write about seeing things and circumstances through God's eyes. It is a fact that we are quick to judge others based on what we see. I was reminded of God's Word that tells us not to be judge or juror, or to be in haste to condemn anyone (Matthew 7:1–6).

Christ came into this world to bring us life and, with that, abundant living. He also did not come to condemn us but to redeem us. He was our example.

Have I ever judged anyone without thinking there may be more to that person's story than I know? Yes, I have. I understand that Christians are prone to making mistakes, just like the ungodly. Therefore, we have God's Word to correct and direct us. The Word of the Lord does not give us room to be carnal thinkers but to be on top of our game.

I started thinking about how others had summarized

me without knowing the complete story. Then I thought about our biblical historians and how they were perceived in people's eyes without knowing God's purpose for their lives.

In the end, the questions should be, Are we fulfilling God's will, or Are we walking outside of his divine plan? Either way, we should start seeing through God's eyes, just as we should have the faith of God. This way of thinking will keep us aligned with our Lord and focused on living a holy life, that which is without questionable doubt.

I aim to see through God's eyes and continue to be a blessing to others as I am blessed.

ACKNOWLEDGMENTS

Lord God, you did it yet again. I want to give honor and recognition to a few select people. I have found that writing this book was an inspiration to me. I was able to look back and re-live some of my life experiences. They all have helped me to see just how the Father has considered me and placed value in me. So my first acknowledgment is given to Jesus.

Stanley, my husband, thanks for the many sermons I have heard you preach over the years. Your messages inspire and give us hope. Thank you for your love and support, and for giving me the space to write this second book. It took away some of our precious time together, but I will make it up in a significant way. And thank you for thirty-nine wonderful years of marriage.

Next, I want to thank my good friend Sandra D. North for her friendship over the years. A great woman of God and faithful servant. I have much respect and high expectations for her, Tom, and the family. I value her spiritual eyes and insights. Again, thanks, Sandy, for being there when I needed you.

Bette, Phyllis, and Alicia: Ladies, words cannot express how grateful I am to have you take the time to examine my manuscript. Your input was incredibly valuable in completing this project.

Phyllis, you are a woman of schedule, and when I asked you to assist me, you did not hesitate. Of course I knew that you already had plans, but you fit me in. Thank you.

Alicia, my Philippian neighbor, we are grateful that you and your family are a part of our lives. I enjoy our sofa conversations; they are heartfelt and uplifting. Your enthusiasm to help me was overwhelming.

Bette, though we are miles apart (San Diego, California), I am so grateful that you said yes to my brother many years ago. You have proven to be an incredible asset to our family, and I am sure you are to your friends. I value your librarian knowledge, as you are an avid reader. Happy to get your approval on a book beautifully written.

My aunt, LuVicy Robinson, thank you for helping me piece together the time line of my youth. It's incredible how much I remembered and how much I didn't. Your input was valuable, and I ask God to bless you with good health and strength.

And last, I want to thank my daughter, Sasha; son-in-law, Shaun; and my grandchildren for helping me to value what's important in life: family. I am learning how to show more of God's love, how to listen more, how to rely on God's help more, and most importantly, how to speak God's promises over our lives. And hugs and love go out to my church family, Witness Protection Ministries, Inc., for your continued encouragement and support. God bless you all.

INTRODUCTION

The pessimist sees difficulty in every opportunity.
The optimist sees opportunity in every difficulty.
—Unknown

Where the Lord leads me, I have made up my mind to
follow. Some do not like being told where and when to go
or do certain things. I have heard people say that this is
called "blind trust." They do not like-not being in control;
they want to control every aspect of their lives. They do
not believe that an unseen entity should have that much
control over anyone. I have lived long enough to know that
God knows the end from the beginning. He knows where
we will choose to fall and where we choose to let our faith
arise. So I trust him in all things.

In this book I consider the messages becoming a
powerful tool in our walks with Christ. When we see

others and ourselves through God's eyes, we tend to react to situations differently. The Word of the Lord tells us in Isaiah 55:8 KJV, "For my thoughts are not your thoughts, neither are your ways my ways, saith the Lord."

If we abide in the Almighty, we will see the world and our surroundings in a different light. We will not fall prey to the snares set by the enemy. We will begin to walk more as victors, not as victims. Failures will happen, but they do not define who we will be, just how we allow the failure to determine our outcome.

I remember when I was single, I spent lots of time fasting, praying, and listening to the voice of the Lord. I would sometimes fast for weeks without fail, crying out for the souls of humankind. Not that I do not practice those things now, but back then, I was able to see the world differently. There were no distractions; my focus was different. I did not have the responsibilities I do now. I have moved from one level of maturity to the next. Life events bring about fasting, praying, and listening to the voice of the Lord on an as-needed basis. However, listening to the voice of the Lord and praying is my daily practice. I had good sight but little vision, but that would change as I matured spiritually.

Some of my old coworkers called me an optimist because I tend not to allow negative thoughts to control how I believe. In this way, it kept me away from impure thoughts and unclean actions. I meant to please the Lord and to acknowledge him in all my ideas so that he could direct my steps.

Your takeaway, I hope, from this book should be that of understanding that God's plans are more significant and more considerable for you. And that you can rely on his eyes to see you through all things.

I still have an optimistic point of view coupled with my faith in God. It all keeps me grounded and faithful. Dear Lord, bless each reader, and open their eyes of understanding so they may see your great work and then glorify you even more.

> We learn more from failure than from success.
> Do not let it stop you. Failure builds character.
> —Unknown author

SEE ME THROUGH GOD'S EYES

I will praise thee; for I am fearfully

and wonderfully made:

marvelous are thy works; and that

my soul knoweth right well.

—Psalm 139:14 (KJV)

Have you ever wondered why Christians or only good people say that God cares so much about you? Not focusing on the whole world, just you! What makes you so important to God that he has you on his mind? Your conscience tells you that no one knows you like you know yourself, and you believe it. Weak and vulnerable to failure are a part of who we are, but not without our heavenly Father's help. Without God's assistance, we merely exist, and we do not know the full magnitude of what it is to live. We all need a higher power to teach us and guide us into a better path. So again, I ask, Why does he care so much about you?

Maybe it is because you are unique. Perhaps it is because God has a bigger plan for you. Or maybe it is because God knows that Satan wants to take you down with him to the very depths of hell, where there are only pain, sorrow, grief, loneliness, stress, unforgiveness, hopelessness, and death. You may be wondering, *Don't these things happen to righteous people too?* Yes, it is true, the righteous may experience these as well, but we have the upper hand, we have Jesus Christ, the One who helps us through all our problems. But we can be assured of what the Bible states:

> The thief cometh not, but for to steal, and
> to kill, and to destroy: I am come that they
> might have life, and that they might have it
> more abundantly. (John 10:10 KJV)

I could relate to the statement, Why does God care so much about me? There was a period in my life when I felt unimportant, unvalued, and during those times, I thought that I did not matter much, not much to anybody.

I felt alone, isolated, and unnecessary. But as I matured, I experienced some things, and I found out that God sees me differently. Not the seemingly unnoticed individual but as someone he could love, dote on, cherish, shine through, care for, mold, and most important, save.

> The LORD is my shepherd; I shall not want. He maketh me to lie down in green pastures: he leadeth me beside the still waters. He restoreth my soul: he leadeth me in the paths of righteousness for his name's sake. Yea, though I walk through the valley of the shadow of death, I will fear no evil: for thou art with me; thy rod and thy staff they comfort me. Thou preparest a table before me in the presence of mine enemies: thou anointest my head with oil; my cup runneth over. Surely goodness and mercy shall follow me all the days of my life: and I will dwell in the house of the Lord forever. (Psalm 23:1–6)

The book of Psalms started playing a vital role in my early Christian life. I surrendered my life to Christ at the age of sixteen. I, like King David, praised the Lord in despair; I found Psalms as a place of refuge. I have experienced problems in my life, and those words of restoration, lying down in green pastures, walking through the valley of the shadow of death, fearing no evil, comfort, goodness, and mercy all showed the care of the Father. He was revealing himself to me to be Jehovah-Rohi (the Lord, my shepherd).[1] It was during those times of troubles that I could not see myself through God's eyes. I was hurting too badly. Those psalms kept me inspired, they kept me uplifted, and they even comforted me when I cried at night. Whenever I am asked by anyone for an excellent place to start reading the Bible, I say start with the book of Psalms. I could relate to how King David, when faced with diverse situations, felt as he poured out his soul to the living God and then finding peace in the end. I encourage you to read my first book, *Girls … God's Best 4 U,* and experience God's passion for our young girls and women.

I recall the voice of a young lady named Patrick, who spoke these words to me: "I have been watching you, watched how you handle certain situations, and I have always admired you. You are an inspiration to me." Wow! All these years later, and I can still hear her words echoing through my head. I was speechless. I could think of nothing to answer her with except a thank-you. I did not see myself as an inspiration to anybody, let alone to her. She saw me through God's eyes.

I saw myself through a clouded lens. I could not see the greatness in me, only the silhouette of a young woman moving in a positive direction. I had dreams that I did not understand, yet I knew in the back of my mind that they meant something to my future. More time spent with the Lord cleared my sight; the cloudiness was lifting. With sight, I could only see and trust what was in front of me, and it was limited. Only those things I could control were in my sight. Then Christ began to broaden my vision. One definition of *vision* is something that is foretold by or as if by supernatural means.[2] I learned that I could trust the Lord, and I began to embrace the ideas he placed in me. Some dreams have become realities. I believe the visions that God revealed to me will all come to pass.

Now back to the words Patrick spoke of me: "I have always admired you. You are an inspiration to me." This could not have been possible had I not allowed Christ to be the guide of my life. Pleasing God has always been my highest priority, and it is he who has kept me inspired the most. However, I am grateful that he has placed people in my life I could model. I watched their lives and tried my best to live a meaningful life and to be a great witness for Christ. It all began at home with my parents, my grandmother, my pastor, and others. I looked at all those people. I looked well into their lives, separating the good and the not so good, to see who would be pleasing in God's eyes and who would not. I chose to harvest what would be favorable for me and throw away the unhealthy. I always had God's Word to rely on, and the Holy Ghost would confirm or refute which road I should take. I chose to see my inspirers through the eyes of God, which is how I matured spiritually.

Thank God for surrounding me with real friends with whom we could share our deepest feelings and walk away feeling some sense of freedom. Freedom from the issues of life and freedom to serve others and God with a renewed focus. In each of us, we could see each other as God sees us; victors and children of the Most High.

I wish you would take a moment, stop what you are doing, and know that you are essential. You are someone special. You have value. Not because I say so, but because God sees the real you. See yourself as God sees you. He created a wonderfully made human being called *you*. You are unique, one of a kind, a masterpiece of epic proportions. Do not allow others' opinions to shape, control, and form you into who you do not want to become. Each day when you see yourself in the mirror, view yourself as God sees you.

I want to share something that happened to me many years ago. I was walking into our bedroom, and the Spirit of the Lord said to me, "Look in the mirror and tell me what you see." I walked into the bathroom, looked in the mirror, and replied, "I see a good-looking young lady." Then I walked out. The Spirit of the Lord then said to me, "Go back, and look into the mirror and tell me what you see." I slowly went back into the bathroom with a puzzled look on my face. This time, as I stood there looking, I looked deep into the mirror of my soul. I saw some things that I did not realize were there, and I was amazed. It was then that the Spirit of the Lord said to me, "If you don't like it, I don't like it. Now get rid of it." I knew what he meant. I was so deeply hurt. My stomach got all in a knot, and I began to sob. I saw the real me, and it wasn't pretty.

There were concerns that I had been praying about and believing that God would turn, but I had yet to get an answer. Once I saw what was there, I could see what was hindering my prayers from being answered. I duly noted what I saw, asked God for forgiveness, and moved in the direction of getting rid of them. As you trust God to lead you toward a righteous pathway, he will reveal hidden areas of your life that keep you from moving forward. He not only watches out for our souls, he also wants us to become our best. We are his walking billboards, advertising what Christ will do in the lives of those who commit to and trust him.

When I saw myself through God's eyes, it provoked me to make corrections and guard myself against unhealthy paths that would lead to my destruction. The Lord is always speaking to us, but we get too busy with our own things and fail to hear him. It may be in your heart to do the right things, but you falter along the way and cannot see where you are heading or which direction to take. Stop and take a moment to see yourself, to see what God sees. Make a plan to read the Bible. God will reveal himself to you, and I pray that he opens your eyes so you can see the real you and begin the work of restoration, submission, and complete trust. We will continue to discuss how God sees you in this book.

Lord, help me see myself as you do. I will be chiseled, hammered, and even put through the fire. Every day I am being sculpted and fashioned into a beautifully crafted masterpiece.

You will not destroy me because of your tender mercies and your grace, which make me strong. Please open my eyes, like you did the servant of Elisha, so that I may see the glorious work you are doing in me. For my latter shall be more significant than my former.

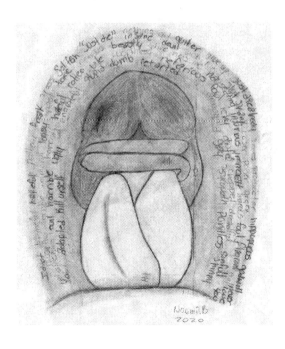

WHERE CAN I GO
BUT TO THE LORD?

For starters, let us say you are a preteen, and you are not sure about much of anything. You are influenced by your friends, and they often say words that hurt you. You do not feel that you can shake it off or share these issues with your parents. So you carry this burden every day.

You are a regular churchgoer because your parents make you. However, you are so preoccupied with "stuff" on your mind that you don't seem to understand or grasp the concepts of what the minister is saying. You may leave the worship service feeling more helpless than before. On the other hand, you might even have tried to reach out to your pastor or Sunday school teacher in search of an answer. But again you walked away feeling unfulfilled and unheard; they did not give you the answer you were seeking. It appeared that they did not seem to understand your concerns.

Gradually these burdens begin to show in ways that are not hard to identify. Your grades are affected, and your attitude may have changed; you are not that happy, jolly person you used to be. You tend to daydream or ignore others when they speak to you. That young mind of yours cannot handle such weight. You do not know it, but you are slowly slipping into a state of depression.

Diana Leagh Matthews, a distant relative of the author of a song I love, shared the story behind it. It was a brief encounter between two men. The author of this song is James Buchanan Coats, born April 16, 1901, in Summerland, Mississippi,[3] and the song is, "Where Could I Go But to the Lord?" Diana writes that James was sitting with a dying neighbor, an old African American man, Mr. Joe Keyes. James asked the neighbor if he knew where he would be spending eternity. Mr. Keyes's reply was, "Where could I go but to the Lord?" Undoubtedly the conversation resonated in James's mind for a while because he wrote the song some years later, in 1940.

I believe that these lyrics are just as prevalent today as in 1940. I think that it can be an answer to some inquiring young minds. It is, "WHERE COULD I GO BUT TO THE LORD?" Here are the lyrics; the words in italics are my summation of the song per line.

Living below in this old sinful world
(*a world without true love*)
Hardly a comfort can afford
(*I want some of the more beautiful things in life*)
Striving alone to face temptation so
(*I feel like I am all alone in this situation*)
Now won't you tell me
(*can anybody tell me what next to do?*)
Where could I go but to the Lord
(*Is this my answer?*)

Where could I go, oh where could I go,
Seeking the refuge for my soul
Needing a friend to save me in the end
Won't you tell me, where could I go but to the Lord[4]

The lyrics imply that when faced with situations that seem overwhelming, we can always turn to the Lord. Mr. Keyes knew this firsthand; he was down to his final hours, yet he held on to the fact that he would spend eternity with the Lord. It also implies to me that maybe he was a God-fearing man who walked the path of righteousness.

So how do you communicate with the Lord? How can you talk with someone you cannot see? The process involves dismissing all other thoughts that are running through your mind and humbly focusing on no one except God. It may be challenging in the beginning because Satan does not want you to get a resolution to your concern. With a repented and broken heart, keep pressing onward. Find a quiet place—your room, your backyard, or even your bathroom. As you began to talk to the Lord in your secret space, begin to tell him your issues and concerns. You will find yourself feeling at ease and open to sharing your problems with him. And never forget to thank him for listening to your prayers. After you pray, wait a moment in silence, still praising God in your mind for helping you. The Lord communicates with us in a calm, soothing voice. His voice speaks peace to your heart, your soul, and your spirit. At that moment, nothing else matters; nothing can harm you now. You have reached the throne room of God. He speaks to your consciousness, and when you hear him, receive his instructions.

Yes, we can always go to the Lord for an answer. If your answer does not come right away, do not be discouraged. He heard your cry, and he will send you a response. Remember when Daniel experienced a disturbing vision, he ate no pleasant bread, no meat, and drank no wine for three full weeks. He prayed and mourned before the Lord, and it was twenty-one days before his answer arrived. Then the most remarkable thing happened to him. An angel came and revealed that for twenty-one days, he was held up by the prince of the kingdom of Persia (demonic spirits), but that Daniel's prayers reached heaven the first day. The angel Michael came to assist Daniel's angel so that his answer would arrive. Read Daniel 10:1–21. The Lord is faithful in answering our prayers. It just requires faith and patience on our parts.

The Lord will always confirm his will for you with his Word. His Word is what he gave us to show just how much he cares. His Word is a culmination of scrolls from over the ages put together to form the book we now know as the Bible. In it, you discover just how precious you are in his eyes and how he sees you.

> Behold, I have graven thee upon the palms
> of my hands. (Isaiah 49:16 KJV)

Keep me as the apple of the eye, hide me under the shadow of thy wings. (Psalm 17:8. KJV)

For thus saith the Lord of hosts; After the glory hath he sent me unto the nations which spoiled you: for he that toucheth you toucheth the apple of his eye. (Zechariah 2:8 KJV)

If you did not quite understand those scriptures from the King James Bible, here are the same verses in the Good News Translation. Same verses with different perspectives.

Jerusalem, I can never forget you! I have written your name on the palms of my hands. (Isaiah 49:16 GNT)

Protect me as you would your very eyes; hide me in the shadow of your wings (Psalm 17:8 GNT)

"Anyone who strikes you strikes what is most precious to me." So the Lord Almighty sent me with this message for the nations

that had plundered his people: (Zechariah
2:8 GNT)

That means a lot. It is saying that God treasures you;
we are his people. He does not like it when someone
hurts you. Christ is tender at heart toward you but firm
enough to bring justice for you. He sees you as a beautifully
constructed person, waiting to be sculptured by his divine
will. Be you younger or older, this chapter of the book is
tailored to help you realize that there is a solution to your
problems. So you see, Jesus does care about you, and you
can always go to him, no matter what.

AVIS D. BROWNLEE-WOOLEY

I AM NOT GOOD ENOUGH

Hold up! Stop right there! Emphatically, halt it right now! Who told you that you are not good enough? What tool are they using to measure you? Are you doing this to yourself? Whose expectations are you trying to meet, theirs or yours? If someone says to you, "What measuring tool are you using to accomplish your goal, because you do not have it in you to do better," do not listen to that negativism. It will only destroy any positive hope in you.

There is greatness in you that is waiting to be tapped into and released. The doorway that releases your greatness is through your faith. The Lord has given everyone the measure of faith. Jesus addressed the disciples by saying,

> And he saith unto them, Why are ye fearful,
> O ye of little faith? Then he arose and

rebuked the winds and the sea, and there
was a great calm. (Matthew 8:26 KJV)

It does not take faith the size of Mount Everest; it only takes faith the size of a mustard seed, the smallest seed on earth. That amount of faith moves mountains. It will help you serve Christ better. You will gain confidence to serve humanity, and that will aid you in achieving your heart's desire. As we submit ourselves humbly before the Lord, his grace will see us through all things.

> For by the grace [of God] given to me I say to every one of you not to think more highly of himself [and of his importance and ability] than he ought to think; but to think so as to have sound judgment, as God has apportioned to each a degree of faith [and a purpose-designed for]. (Romans 12:3 AMP)

Now we explore this type of lack of confidence played out in the life of someone from biblical history—Moses. A Hebrew by birth but raised as the son of Pharaoh, and who did not know his rightful place, was faced with two of his biggest challenges: (1) to believe in a God he knew not of, and (2) to confront his past, the people who raised him. He could not see what God saw in him. Consequently, the best way out, he thought, was to find excuses when God spoke to him out of a burning bush.

Moses was raised in a prominent family, the house of Pharaoh. He had the best of the best: best education, best health plan, the best choice of women, the best selection of clothing and food, and so on. Moses' life was one of mystery and came to fulfill God's plan for such a time as this. (Read the second chapter of Exodus regarding the birth of Moses). After killing an Egyptian, he fled Egypt and sought refuge in a strange land among strange people. And yet, at one point in his life, when God wanted to work through him, he started making excuses. He stated the obvious, that he felt not good enough. His measuring tool was fear; it was self-inflicted. He experienced doubt that the conflicts in his past would halt him from obeying God. And that his shortcoming would be enough to deter God from asking him to do what he thought was an impossible task. Let us listen to Moses' conversation with God.

And Moses answered and said, But, behold, they will not believe me, nor hearken unto my voice: for they will say, The Lord hath not appeared unto thee.

And the Lord said unto him, what is that in thine hand? And he said A rod.

And he said, Cast it on the ground. And he cast it on the ground, and it became a serpent, and Moses fled from before it.

And the Lord said unto Moses, Put forth thine hand, and take it by the tail. And he put forth his hand and caught it, and it became a rod in his hand:

That they may believe that the LORD God of their fathers, the God of Abraham, the God of Isaac, and the God of Jacob, appeared unto thee.

And the Lord said furthermore unto him, Put now thine hand into thy bosom. And he put his hand into his bosom: and when he took it out, behold, his hand was leprous as snow.

And he said, Put thine hand into thy bosom again. And he put his hand into his bosom again; and plucked it out of his bosom, and, behold, it was turned again as his other flesh.

And it shall come to pass, if they will not believe thee, neither hearken to the voice of the first sign, that they will believe the voice of the latter sign.

And it shall come to pass, if they will not believe also these two signs, neither hearken unto thy voice, that thou shalt take of the water of the river, and pour it upon the dry land: and the water which thou takest out of the river shall become blood upon the dry land.

And Moses said unto the Lord, O my Lord, I am not eloquent, neither heretofore, nor since thou hast spoken unto thy servant: but I am slow of speech and of a slow tongue.

And the Lord said unto him, Who hath made man's mouth? Or who maketh the dumb, or deaf, or the seeing, or the blind? Have not I the Lord?

Now therefore go, and I will be with thy mouth, and teach thee what thou shalt say.

And he said, O my Lord, send, I pray thee, by the hand of him whom thou wilt send.

And the anger of the Lord was kindled against Moses, and he said, Is not Aaron the Levite, thy brother? I know that he can speak well. And also, behold, he cometh forth to meet thee: and when he seeth thee, he will be glad in his heart.

And thou shalt speak unto him and put words in his mouth: and I will be with thy mouth, and with his mouth, and will teach you what ye shall do.

And he shall be thy spokesman unto the people: and he shall be, even he shall be to thee instead of a mouth, and thou shalt be to him instead of God.

And thou shalt take this rod in thine
hand, wherewith thou shalt do signs.
(Exodus 4:1–17 KJV)

After Moses listed a string of excuses, God still wanted
to use him. God could have chosen someone else, but
Moses was the right man for the task. Moses was favored
by Pharaoh while living in the palace, and he had always
found favor with God in and out of the palace. Don't you
know God was aware of Moses' weaknesses? With those
weaknesses, God would provide a way out of no way. He
led the children out of Egypt through the Red Sea across
on dry grounds, fed his people when there was no food to
be found, and delivered water in a dry place. God would
perform miracles by the hands of Moses. God's plans were
far more significant than Moses could fathom.

This dialogue between God and Moses might remind
you of yourself at some point in your life, when the Lord
spoke to you about doing something. You came up with all
types of reasons not to be assigned the task. When your flaws
and issues are hindering you, don't let them hold you back
from accepting the challenge. In addition, don't you know
that God is aware that you may have even taken a life? He

has considered all things, yet there is still room for you at the cross. If you only think inside the box, you are unaware that you will come in contact with someone who will need your story of destruction, salvation, and deliverance. You are good enough to carry the torch of salvation because the Lord will make you worthy. The Lord is merciful and just, long-suffering, patient, and forgiving. We should be no one's judge when it comes to eternity.

Though the Lord showed Moses all those signs, he still refused to believe that I Am could use someone with flaws and issues, and that nothing was impossible for him to do. The Lord wanted to free his people from four hundred years of bondage, but he also wanted Moses to realize that when he was willing to align himself with I Am, the possibilities were endless. The same applies to us. As we align ourselves with Jesus, the limitations are off. We tend to forget who we are: heirs and joint heirs with Christ:

> And if children, then heirs; heirs of God and joint-heirs with Christ; if so be that we suffer with him, that we may also be glorified together. (Romans 8:17 KJV)

THROUGH GOD'S EYES I

But most important, I believe that El Elyon (the Most High God), El Shaddai (Lord God Almighty), and Elohim (God of power and might), wanted to show the magnitude of his existence against a ruler who considered himself to be a god.

Christ knows our weaknesses and our strengths: he knows because he created us. You must not see yourself as a hopeless being. Seek the good in you; everybody has some. Focus on those positive things, and ask God to help you build them up to become a talking piece between God and Satan. Job did not have low self-esteem, but he was an upright man who feared God (reverenced and respected). We see how Job's life plays out when Satan approached God about testing him.

> One day the angels came to present themselves before the LORD, and Satan also came with them. The LORD said to Satan, "Where have you come from?" Satan answered the LORD, "From roaming throughout the earth, going back and forth on it." Then the LORD said to Satan, "Have you considered my servant Job? There is no one on earth

like him; he is blameless and upright, a man who fears God and shuns evil." "Does Job fear God for nothing?" Satan replied. "Have you not put a hedge around him and his household and everything he has? You have blessed the work of his hands so that his flocks and herds are spread throughout the land. But now stretch out your hand and strike everything he has, and he will surely curse you to your face." The LORD said to Satan, "Very well, then, everything he has is in your power, but on the man, himself do not lay a finger." Then Satan went out from the presence of the LORD. (Job 1:6–12 NIV)

What a fantastic proposal! God and Satan having a conversation about you. Though Job was tested, in the end he recognized that God was the source of everything he owned. Job turned his faith back to God, and in turn, God restored everything that was lost, double for his troubles. For the sake of time, read Job chapter 42 in its entirety. See how Job repented and prayed for his friends, and then

Jehovah Tsidkenu (The Lord Our Righteousness) restored unto him everything that was lost.

God knows that you are capable of greatness in many ways. Do not undermine your abilities. Do not count yourself out before you get started. Right out of the batting cage, Moses began using his shortcomings as tools to abate achieving a task that God had for him. He chose fear when the Hebrew slaves reminded him of his action, killing an Egyptian. Fulfilling God's command would not only demonstrate God's miraculous power, it would display how following God's directions will make us champions.

The power to choose strength over weakness and faith over fear is our measuring tools. These are the things that make us good enough. God will never give us a task and not have given us the tools to accomplish it. We are as weak as we think, and we are as strong as we believe. Proverbs 23:7a (KJV) states, "For as he thinketh in his heart, so is he."

The "he" refers to us, a man, or humanity. You can do all things by the strength of the Lord. He enables and equips you daily with benefits that will guide you in fulfilling the task set before you—becoming that champion he knows you to be. What God saw in Moses to make him good enough was a strong tower with a speech impediment. God saw a one-time murderer as a strong spiritual leader with qualities that would satisfy I Am. And a man of compassion who would care for his people in difficult times.

As you look around at people, especially those close to you, you may see their strengths and shortcomings. Just as you may see theirs, they may see yours. Take time and intercede for them; include them in your daily devotions. Furthermore, this should not stop you from wanting to see yourself as God sees you. Embrace the tools of faith and hope. Then and only then can you see yourself as good enough.

WILL I EVER GET THERE?

Every day an elite group of people strive to be just a little better than the day before; they make it a priority. Then there are those—the majority—who just settle in and live their lives as if nothing will get better. I can hear the voice of Joyce Myers saying, "Battlefield of the Mind"[5] it is where the process starts and where it all ends. We are in spiritual warfare every day, whether we know it or not. Satan attacks the places that govern our actions: the mind, the heart. Gaining access to this portal is crucial. He once was an angel of truth and is very much aware of the operations of humanity. He knows the power behind our thoughts. We are what we think we are, and we have what we believe we have. These are fighting words to him. Thus, the Word of the Lord tells us in Proverbs 4:23 (KJV), "Keep thy heart with all diligence; for out of it are the issues of life."

When you allow Satan to get into your head, he causes havoc. You lose the sense of reality. Doubt sets in, and you begin feeling that you will never get to the place of your dreams. Hopelessness is your daily bread when you drink from the cup of doubt.

Further abusing yourself, you put yourself under the microscope of life and look for every bug, virus, infection, and malignancy without seeing the cure. And the cure is known as Jesus, the Christ, the Son of the living God." He has created and provided so many ways to better ourselves while remaining true to who we want to become. My pastor calls this Bible verse the "themes of thought":

> Finally, brethren, whatsoever things are true, whatsoever things are honest, whatsoever things are just, whatsoever things are pure, whatsoever things are lovely, whatsoever things are of good report; if there be any virtue, and if there be any praise, think on these things. (Philippians 4:8 KJV)

Still thinking that you won't get there? I would like to believe in this manner. Your life is like a book being written.

First comes the thought and then the draft. You create an outline of what your topics are going to be, and then you start writing sentences that make up the paragraphs related to your topic. All the while it is being written, there will be lots of corrections and changes. There will be many scribblings sideways, in and out of margins, drawing lines through sentences that may not make sense, writing, and rewriting. In this manner, anyone reading the final story will follow and understand its meaning.

Isn't this true of us, the basis of becoming that champion? From conception until your birth, your parents' main goal was to take care of this helpless infant. They fed you, loved on you, and provided protection for you, hoping that they would raise you right (the draft and the outlines). They watched you form your first words, take your first steps, and become independent. All along the way, you are making little mistakes. But it's okay because you were in the training stage of becoming who you are purposed to be (the sentences and the paragraphs). Once out of the protection of your parents, you began to establish yourself. At this time, you started to make choices and hard decisions; some will be good and some will not (scribbling in and out of margins). You try to learn from your mistakes, but sometimes find yourself a repeat offender (writing and rewriting). Then at some point in life, you find your purpose, start maturing in it. Now you can say the book is ready to be read by anyone. You have gotten the kinks, so to speak, all worked out. You are walking in your destiny and are now able to become a blessing to someone else along his or her journey.

God wants you to see yourself. You are a blank canvas, yet beautifully made, experiencing the thing called life. And along the way, the choices you make will help shape who you are becoming. You realize that you are a masterpiece in progress. The rod of correction and the staff of direction (the Word of the Lord) help you refocus on the goal that will lead you into your purpose.

When I was so noticeably young I scarcely remember, our father and grandfather built us a home. It had three bedrooms, a living room, front and back porches, and a small kitchen and dining room. The boys had the smallest room of all. The girls had the largest; no dividers separated it, just one prominent place. Of course, seven girls slept there, and sometimes my youngest brother. One cold night in January 1962, after our father had gone to work at the ITT Rayonier, there was a house fire. I had to be between five and six years old. Our oldest brother, Oscar, went to spend the night at a relative's home. This left only George, the third oldest, and two-year-old Denver, the youngest brothers at home. We all had retired for the evening. George told me that he decided to sleep that night on the floor in our parents' room. He did tell me why, but I cannot recall.

Also in that room was the family dog, Lady. George said that while everyone was asleep, Lady started barking, jumping up and down, and then on our parents' bed. It woke him up. He noticed the smoke coming from the wall above our mother's head. He sprang to his feet while calling out for Momma. It was an electrical fire. She told him to get everybody up and out of the house. He woke up my sisters and instructed them to bring somebody with them and get in the car. Well I knew it was an uneven number in the room; somebody just panicked out of the calamity. I wonder to this day why someone didn't yell at me or pull me up. My bed was near the doorway. Maybe they did try. Nevertheless, they left me. Looking back at this event, it was all a part of God's master plan. Everyone was in the car, but right before our mother pulled off, George remembered and told her, "Avis isn't here!" He ran back into an intensely burning house, pulled me by my top plat, and ran out. I remember waking up seeing the back of his white T-shirt as he was running out, and the house filled with smoke. I ran out, not feeling the heat or affected by the smoke. This last thing I remembered was the moment I stepped off the final step leading away from the house, the roof caved in.

Some years ago, George and I were talking about the incident and how it all unfolded. Yes, I said, I remember the roof of the house caving in when I took the last step. He stopped me and said, "Tate (that was his nickname for me), don't you remember, the house exploded when you stepped out? I told him no. Remember, I was only five or six years old. But I remembered our father always kept large containers of kerosene on the front and sometimes on the back porch. Maybe that was why the explosion happened and accelerated the fire. Once we were all safely loaded in the car, our mother pulled out, and off we went to our grandparents' home.

Our father returned home when word reached him. The house was all destroyed, burned down to ashes by the time he got home. I found out later that the house was consumed in fewer than ten minutes. Our father told me, before he fell asleep in the presence of the Lord, that during the panic, no one informed him that we were all safe. So when he saw the devastation, he thought that he lost his whole family. Later that same day, we found the charred remains of Lady. Thank God that he led George to sleep in our parents' room that night and that Lady was there watching over the family.

Just a sidebar: I remember our last Christmas there. We got lots of toys. Denver and I spent much time playing with his toy cars in our living room as we watched the *Flintstones*. I recall that later, at our grandparents' home, we children were more concerned about our Christmas things being destroyed than being alive. Remember, this was the thought of a five- or six-year-old.

My father never ceased to tell me that I was the blessed child, the seventh, like himself. I always played it down, but as the years rolled on, I began to understand that he was right. It does not make me more significant than the remaining siblings, but simply that God's plan for me is a one-off. I love my family; our diverse personalities reflect how beautifully and wonderfully we are made. Additionally, it shows God's goodness toward us, and our diversity brings us together in a unique way.

God's purpose and plan for my life would not allow Satan to destroy me. I believe they had a conversation about me before I was a glimmer in my parents' thoughts. I have been tested at many junctures of my life, but I will always remain faithful to my Savior. I am a singer and a writer, two of the gifts that bring me into my purpose. I know Christ has shown me other gifts, and only time will see me fulfill them.

Jesus knows the end from the beginning. Just like he has plans for me, you are no different. He has laid out blueprints with your name on them and is waiting to give you an expected end. I am thankful that my life is meaningful and still a work in progress. I cannot see the full scope of what I am becoming, but I know that if I remain faithful to God and his divine will, all is well.

We are all born wonderfully made with the potential to become our utmost. Be steadfast and unmovable. The Lord will help you get there. Everyone's road to getting there is not the same. Continue to seek the Lord concerning his will for your life. Watch, listen, and pray without ceasing. Then you can say as I do that you will get there. And believe me, the result will be marvelous!

SAMSON AND DELILAH.

STAY IN THE LIGHT

Thy word is a lamp unto my feet,

and a light unto my path.

—Psalm 119:105

I was watching a movie one evening, and as the good guys were trying to escape, one character said to the others, "Stay in the light." If they stayed in the light, the adversary could not harm them. That rang a sweet tune in my spirit, "Stay in the light." No matter what you deal with, stay in the light.

God's Word tells us that being in the light gives us a clear pathway. You can see clearly who you are and where you are going. You can even see the enemy coming from a distance. If we stay in the light, Satan can be spotted and recognized by the way he dresses, the way he thinks, and the way he talks. Do not be fooled; he comes in sheep's clothing to trick anyone into believing that he is genuine and righteous.

> Beware of false prophets, which come to you in sheep's clothing, but inwardly they are ravening wolves. (Matthew 7:15 KJV)

That is Satan's nature; he is a liar and the father of lies.

> You belong to your father, the devil, and you want to carry out your fathers' desires. He was a murderer from the beginning, not holding to the truth, for there is no truth in him. When he lies, he speaks his native language, for he is a liar and the father of lies. (John 8:44 NIV)

How many worshippers of the true and living God have been tricked into believing Satan's lies? Countless people stepped away from the lit path and found themselves in trouble and darkness. I examine four of these people who failed God, yet he did not turn his back on them. He always has a purpose and a plan for us, and a way out, leading us back into the light. It is so beautiful having the Holy Spirit watch out for us. The Holy Spirit shows the magnitude of love that our heavenly Father has for humanity.

Let us start with Adam and Eve in the garden of Eden. About these two people, much can be said. First, they were the first humans created by almighty God. They were wonderfully made, without spot or wrinkle, made in the image of God. They were set amid a beautiful, harmonious environment where the universe, humans, and animals were in agreement. Not a care in the world. I can imagine them having conversations with God every day in the cool of the evenings; these must have been the highlights of their days.

Second, during one of those conversations, God gave them specific directives to enjoy the beautiful place prepared for them but not to indulge in the tree amid the garden, the tree of the knowledge of good and evil. God said that eating the fruit from this tree would bring death.

Satan, once an angelic being, was son of the morning. He dwelt in heaven and was in God's presence always. He was a beautifully made angel. He had everything going for him until he decided to become like the Most High. He wanted to exalt his throne above the stars of God, sit upon the mount of the congregation in the sides of the north, and ascend above the heights of the clouds. These positions were reserved for almighty God only. Right then, everything in heaven changed. Satan could not be like the Most High, and he and other angels who followed his way of thinking were kicked out of heaven, down into the earth. This event all took place before God spoke everything into existence. Read Isaiah 14:12–17; Ezekiel 28:13–19; Genesis 1:1–2.

So now Satan, the fallen angel, saw an opportunity to defy God. He disguised himself in a snake form and used part of God's Word to trick Eve into believing that God did not mean they would die. Satan said to Eve, "Ye shall not surely die," (Genesis 3:4 KJV) as if God was hiding something from them. Satan continued, "For God know that in the day ye eat thereof, then your eyes shall be opened, and ye shall be as gods, knowing good and evil" (Genesis 3:5 KJV). What did they know about being a god? The subliminal message planted in her head was Satan's wish: to be a god. They had everything in Eden that they would ever need. They had almighty God to commune with daily, peace and harmony, and a glorious dwelling to inhabit. The temptation was too great of an opportunity for her to miss. The fruit from the tree also became attractive and delicious looking. Upon sharing it with Adam, something happened, not as they supposed.

It was something out of the ordinary, and the change that overtook them was not good. When God created man and woman, he gave them free will. Instead of continuing to trust God, the One who created them, they chose to use their free will by disobeying God. In my eyes, Adam and Eve were, in a manner of speaking, innocent, mere babies so easily influenced. Satan's tactic worked. He caused Adam and Eve to disobey God, and in doing so, God pronounced judgment upon the serpent, the woman, and the man.

Before they could do more damage by eating from the tree of life, they lost access to heaven on earth, Eden, the one place where everything made sense and where freedom existed. God evicted them, sending them away to live out their punishment, but not without providing them with clothes and instructions on what to do next. Their choice not only brought about physical death to them, but it alienated them and all humanity from the light, and they found themselves in the darkness of sin. Therefore, we are all born into sin. Humanity will need a Savior to bring us back into the light. This is what Christ's death at Calvary provided. Genesis chapters 2 and 3 give you all the insights into this couple.

Now let us take a look at Samson, the ruler and judge of the children of Israel for twenty years. A man of God who had the favor of God, faltered significantly, and in the end, found redemption. Samson was unbelievably strong and quite handsome. Before he was conceived, God gave his barren mother specific instructions on what not to do and told his father, Manoah, how Samson should be raised. Mom was not to drink wine or strong drink and not to eat any unclean food. No razor should touch his head for he will be a Nazarite unto God. As Samson grew, God's spirit was with him.

Moreover, Samson loved women outside his race, and the choice of women he would love would cause a rift between the people he ruled and his parents. He married a woman from Timnath, a daughter of the Philistines, the enemy of the children of Israel. He was not well-liked among the rulers of Philistine. During the wedding feast, he gave a riddle to the men of Timnath that they were to solve in seven days. Samson's wife was coerced into revealing the answer to his riddle; the men of Timnath threatened to kill her and burn her father's home. Samson was confident they would not guess the answer, and when he found out that it was revealed, he became angry. Therefore, he had to fulfill the promise if they answered correctly. His wife and father-in-law were killed sometime after that. After his wife's untimely death, Samson went on a killing spree, further infuriating his enemies.

Samson retreated to the rocks of Etam. There, the men of Judah approached him about turning himself in for fear of the Philistines who ruled them. He agreed. The Philistines sent an army of men to bring in Samson, and his anger intensified when he discovered they were planning to kill him. Samson killed a thousand men with the jawbone of a donkey.

He later met another woman, Delilah, and fell in love. Can you see yourself or someone you know in this scenario? She pressed him on many occasions regarding the source of his strength. Samson eventually failed God when he chose to share the source of his power with Delilah. I would compare it to playing with fire; ultimately you get burned. That is what happened to Samson. Satan deceived Samson through his weaknesses, which were beautiful women. When Samson finally gave Delilah the correct source of his strength, she cut off his hair, and Samson's strength was gone. In the end, Samson lost his eyesight and was shamed and used as a sport for his captures. I do not believe that anyone noticed, but Samson's hair began to grow. You won't find it in the scriptures, but I think Samson felt confident that God would give his strength back and hear his prayer one more time. What Delilah took away was now restored. Samson did turn back to God, and God did answer his prayer. Samson died with his enemies, the Philistines.

Nonetheless, Samson killed more in his death than he did while he lived. He lived in physical darkness because he left the lighted pathway. All the while, Elohim had a plan for Samson's life. You can find the fascinating story of Samson in Judges chapters 13 through 16.

Last, King David. Before he was king, David was a shepherd boy, tending his father's sheep. The prophet Samuel came looking for the next king among the sons of Jesse and found the one that God would anoint. Young David watched over his father's sheep with great care, and his faith in the true and living God was strong. On two occasions, his faith would lead him to kill a lion and a bear as they took one of his father's sheep. These events were a prelude for what would come to be in David's life a (1) test of will and a (2) test of his faith in God. As time would have it, after defeating Goliath and driving the evil spirits away from King Saul through his music, David was elevated in rank and eventually became the new king of Israel.

However, Satan would not allow an opportunity to pass without getting into the picture. King David had many wives, and lusting after other women provided Satan that opportunity. King David had a man killed, Uriah, because he fell in love and impregnated this man's wife. I sometimes wonder how God could still use David after all his issues. Aren't we supposed to be better than this? We followers of the True and living God should set higher standards than carnal man. Then I am reminded of this one important fact about King David: He was a man after God's own heart.

> Then the people asked for a king, and he gave them Saul son of Kish, of the tribe of Benjamin, who ruled forty years.
>
> After removing Saul, he made David their king. God testified concerning him: "I have found David son of Jesse, a man after my own heart; he will do everything I want him to do." (Acts 13:21–22 KJV)

Whenever David sinned, he went to God and asked and received forgiveness. He would sing songs of praise to the God of his fathers and always exalted the Lord. These acts of worship are what our Lord wants to see in our lives. With all our failures, we still must repent and worship our Savior. Keeping us in the lit pathway of Jehovah El-Roi (the God who sees me) is God's divine plan.

David wanted to build the house of the Lord, but God said no because David had too much blood on his hands; he was a man of war. It would be David's son, Solomon, who would build God's temple.

> Then he said to Solomon his son and charged him to build an house for the Lord God of Israel.
>
> And David said to Solomon, My son, as for me, it was in my mind to build an house unto the name of the Lord my God:
>
> But the Word of the Lord came to me saying, Thou hast shed blood abundantly, and hast made great wars: thou shalt not build an house unto my name, because thou hast shed much blood upon the earth in my sight.

Behold, a son shall be born to thee who
shall be a man of rest; and I will give him
rest from all his enemies round about: for
his name shall be Solomon, and I will give
peace and quietness unto Israel in his days.

He shall build an house for my name, and
he shall be my son, and I will be his father,
and I will establish the throne of his kingdom
over Israel forever. (1 Chronicles 22:6–10 KJV)

King David walked away from the light on many occasions,
but he always seemed to repent, sought God's face, offered up
sacrifices, and exalted and praised his God. The Lord would
forever forgive him, regardless of the harsh punishments he
meted out to David. Read 2 Samuel 16 through 1 King 2 and
you will find King David's tumultuous family life.

Okay, let us bring it into the present day. What about
you? How many times have you walked away from the
light of Christ and found yourself wandering in darkness?
Do not tend to notice others' faults and close your eyes
to your flaws. We can be quick to judge others so harshly
without an understanding heart and an objective frame
of mind. The Bible says not to be too ready to pronounce

judgment for the mote in someone's eye when there is a beam protruding from your eye. It is quite easy to blame everyone else when it comes to explaining why you fell short. Leaving the lighted path is costly. It not only can bring separation, it can bring death.

Look to the Lord God; he wants to keep you in the lit pathway. Let him become to you Jehovah Jireh (your provider). He is Jehovah Shalom (the Lord of peace). Let him become Elohim (God, the Creator, powerful and mighty, Lord of lords). He is El-Roi (the strong One who sees). He is Yahweh-Shemmah (the Lord, who is present). And he wants to be so much more to us, proving just how much we can trust him to keep us in the light.

If you are already in the light, great. Stay there. But if you have strayed from the light, come back; there is only death and destruction waiting for you. Adam and Eve, Samson, and King David all were creations of God but failed in their trust and patience. What will be your epitaph? He or she stayed on the righteous pathway and was a great example of Christ's love. Or will it be one of sorrow and grief? Repentance and asking God for forgiveness are necessities for Christians. Continue to let the Lord be a lamp unto your feet and a light unto your path.

GREATER IS HE WHO IS IN ME THAN HE WHO IS IN THE WORLD

Another pandemic has hit the world, one that many have not seen the likes of since the 1918 flu pandemic. The villain is COVID-19, one of the coronaviruses. It has similarities to the earlier pandemic, except in the 1918 pandemic, its victims could be dead within hours after contracting the virus.[6]

Every day the first matter on the news was and often continues to be about the coronavirus pandemic. All day, throughout the day, we are fed this daily. We have sensed fear creep its way into the hearts of people. Everyone has been getting educated on how this virus affects our usual ways of life. But without any known cure at hand and the methods by which it spreads, some people's reactions were cavalier. Everything was changing so fast. Most people took it seriously, while others tested the validity of its severity. But as the pandemic moved among the skeptics, everyone began to seek ways of sheltering themselves and their loved ones.

It was great to hear updates of how, when, and where the virus hit, who was affected, and the efforts to get people tested. But over time, it was becoming information overload, primarily because the daily information, being given by our experts and president, was changing daily. This sudden change in lifestyle was something new. Scrambling experts are still trying to get a handle on what information is deemed as correct. It shook the globe. Again, it was causing panic and skepticism among many. I am reminded what the Word of the Lord said:

> For nation shall rise against nation, and kingdom against kingdom: and there shall be famines, and pestilences, and earthquakes, in divers places.
>
> All these are the beginning of sorrows. (Matthew 24:7–8 KJV)

Humanity has experienced pandemics since the beginning of time. Here are a few.

1. The ten plagues by the hand of Moses against Pharaoh and the Egyptians. The types of plagues - water turned into blood; frogs, lice, swarms of flies; death of all four-legged animals; boils with blains; hail; locusts; and three days of darkness. The final plague was the firstborn of every Egyptian, humans and beasts, died by the hand of death angels. The death toll is unknown[7].

2. Plague of Justinian (541–542), the bubonic plague, led to a death toll of between 25 and 100 million, equaling 40 to 50 percent of the European population[8].

3. The Japanese smallpox epidemic (735–737), with a death toll of two million, equaling one third of the Japanese people[9].

4. The sixth cholera pandemic (1899–1923), with 800,000 deaths of European, Asian, and African populations[10].

5. All the pandemics wiped out sizable numbers of people and animals young and old.

I recall a movie I saw in which the villain set out to destroy a sizable number of the population, a purging to get rid of humanity's impurities. He was successful in his goal, but not for long. Good triumphed in the end, restoring what was lost, and uniting humanity with surprising strength and courageous resilience.

What happened in the movie and how events are unfolding in real life are identical. The villain is COVID-19, and the good guys are everyday people, including the people of the living God. Satan aims to destroy all by any means necessary. However, God will not allow Satan and COVID-19 to destroy the world.

We have lost many souls, those of the ungodly and those of the righteous. So where can I go to be safe? There is no magical place one can go and hide from this deadly virus. Find safety in the family of God. Outside of his protection, the odds are not favorable. If you die outside the safety of Jesus, the punishment after death is far greater. The righteous will spend eternity with Christ, but the ungodly will spend eternity in hell with Satan and his angels. For the righteous, we put our confidence in these words of Christ:

Let not your heart be troubled: ye believe in God, believe also in me.

> In my Father's house are many mansions: if it were not so, I would have told you. I go to prepare a place for you.
>
> And if I go and prepare a place for you, I will come again, and receive you unto myself; that where I am, there ye may be also. (John 14:1–3 KJV)

These catastrophes do not occur without God's awareness. I believe that God allows events like what is happening today, and in the world's history, for humanity to see and know that God is God of all, and without him, there is no safety in this world. It is beautiful when we band together to fight against an enemy that knows no boundaries and does not discriminate against race, social status, or wealth. It's all about watching out for not only yourself but becoming your brothers' keeper, a good sign of undying unity.

With widespread panic, financial ruin, and hopelessness, the world, as we now know, is forced to rely on science and technology. People are looking for our government to solve their crisis. Science has its place in helping us solve issues that pertain to our way of living, and our government is there to help us maintain order. We Christians understand and believe that our help and ultimate trust comes from the Lord and not through humankind.

So what are the Christians doing to aid the situation during this pandemic? The Christians are not allowed to congregate in houses of worship for a season. And at best, only minimal numbers—usually ten or fewer—can worship in a sanctuary. Social distance is the new normal, but we have found that there are other ways of assembling without involving physical contact. If we look through God's eyes, we will seek his face and the answer that best fits our lives and ministry. This is what most ministries are trying.

Live streaming in many forms are more popular than before. We are continuing to spread the Gospels of Christ through these means. We are restoring hope, peace, and salvation, reaching more non-churchgoers than before. People panic because of the known and the unknown, and that is why the Christians are to stay ready and be available when these things happen.

And Jesus answered and said unto them, Take heed that no man deceive you.

> For many shall come in my name, saying, I am Christ; and shall deceive many. (Matthew 24:4–5 KJV)

* * *

> Verily, verily, I say unto you, He that believeth on me, the works that I do shall he do also; and greater works than these shall he do; because I go unto my Father.
>
> And whatsoever ye shall ask in my name, that will I do, that the Father may be glorified in the son.
>
> If ye shall ask any thing in my name, I will do it.
>
> If ye love me, keep my commandments.
>
> Peace I leave with you, my peace I give unto you: not as the world giveth, give I unto you. Let not your heart be troubled, neither let it be afraid. (John 14:12–15, 27 KJV)

Even though our country should learn from errors of the past, when it comes to epidemics, it appears that those in power were slow to react, creating discord among leaders, nationally and around the globe. As stated earlier, our hope and trust should be invested in the Lord Jesus Christ and not in humankind. God never fails, but people do. We should pray for our leaders and continue to remain faithful to our God.

I am a medical laboratory scientist and a Christian, and sometimes I find myself questioning why the good is suffering with the bad. I know that the Lord promised that he would never leave us or forsake us. That is my takeaway, his promise to me. God is good at his promises, and I should trust in that alone.

> Ye are of God, little children, and have overcome them: because greater is he that is in you, than he that is in the world. (1 John 4:4 KJV)

Evaluating how precious our time on earth is, I realize that having Christ in my life supersedes everything around me. I do not take it for granted that the virus is real and that people are dying daily. I must keep my faith and trust in the Lord, knowing that death will come to us all, and we must be spiritually ready to face death with peace. Also, to be confident where will we spend eternity, heaven or hell.

Jesus's death on the cross gave us all another chance to be reconnected to the Father and to provide us with peace. Adam's and Eve's decisions to disobey God alienated us all from the Creator. Christ's death and resurrection put the final stamp on attaining victory over death. Christians no longer live in fear of death because of what Christ did for the believers.

I awakened one morning before dawn thinking about the things that were troubling me. I got up and prayed; I needed God's direction. Over the years I have learned that I can take my cares directly to the Lord and leave them there. Do I ever think about them again? Yes. Do I ever get impatient and try to solve the issue myself? Sometimes. Ultimately, I come to my senses and realize that in my strength, I can solve nothing. So I take my problems to him and leave them there. Then I heard the voice of the Lord telling me that all is well. He asked me, "Do you trust me?" My answer was yes. Then he said, "I see the big picture; I know the end from the beginning. Be patient, and know that I am God and that I will solve your problems." I got up confident, knowing that I had nothing to worry about.

Seeing through the eyes of God involves trust, faith, patience, and hope. Trust that you can rely on his Word to come through for you. Faith in him that what he has done for others he can do for you and with a more excellent outcome. Patience to not move ahead of his divine will. And hope that keeps it all alive, looking into a dimly lit future and believing that trust, faith, and patience were not for nothing. We must all remember that greater is he who is in us than he who is in the world.

KILLER Bs

Have you ever been stung by a bee? I, like so many others, have been stung on many occasions. One bee sting is torture, but multiple stings can be life-threatening. The pain seems to go on for days. It is an unpleasant experience. Nothing tends to console you until you get relief. If the stinger isn't removed, the site swells, hardens, and continues to cause pain to the site. Some people are allergic to the bee venom, and it can cause death if not treated in time.

We all have heard of this old saying, "If it ain't one thing, it's another." This statement tends to be right in the lives of many. They do not see a way out, and when they see a glimmer of hope, something happens, and *poof*, there goes the dream. Troubled on every side, distressed, and without hope. Just the opposite of what the Bible tells the believers.

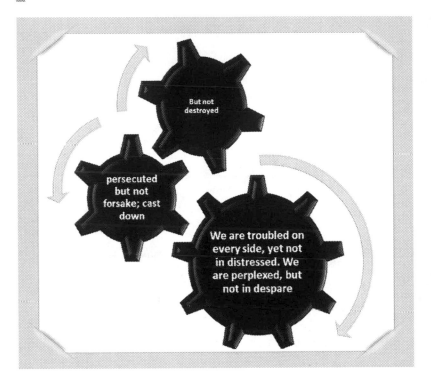

2 Corinthians 4: 8–9 KJV

Just when you think things cannot get any worse, the bottom drops out. During the pandemic in America, there arose some killer bees in Washington State. The hype had many in an uproar. Could things get any worse? We are dealing with this virus, and now here come the bees!

Some experts say that the bees were not a considerable threat to humans but to other types of bees and animals. Can you imagine being a regular bee, just buzzing right along, doing your bee diligence, and there comes a bigger bee, engulfing you and finally killing you. Awful, this is just awful. Here is the picture of how the Bs of life can suffocate and destroy you. They sneak up on you, and before you know it, you have become another statistic. Our heavenly Father wants us to be strong and vigilant, not overtaken by the adversary.

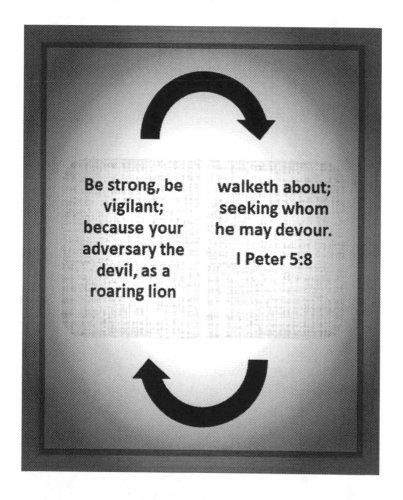

Be strong, be vigilant; because your adversary the devil, as a roaring lion walketh about; seeking whom he may devour.

I Peter 5:8

Standing strong and vigilant is not a one-time command that we do but a continuous defense cycle. Satan and his demonic angels are always on the prowl. We should not drop our guard at any time. Satan does not miss an opportunity to destroy all possible hope, kill the very life that God has breathed into us, or steal the visions and dreams placed within us from conception. The love of our Father is so strong and pure that it hurts him deeply when we fail. But remember he said that he would never leave us or forsake us. And with that same failure, he makes a way of escape.

> There hath no temptation taken you but such as is common to man, but God is faithful who will not suffer you to be tempted above that ye are able; but will with the temptation also make a way to escape, that ye may be able to bear it. (1 Corinthians 10:13 KJV)

As stated earlier, beestings are painful, but they do not last forever. The bad Bs spoken over us are painful, but they do not have to continue throughout our lifetimes. Do not allow the bad Bs to decompose, swell, and harden your heart against God and to what he can do for you. He wants to treat you before it is too late.

Some of the descriptions below will not begin with the letter B, but their negative meanings nevertheless still hold so many captives. This form of captivity can destroy any possibility of encouraging hope and change. These Bs and negative words are not healthy for anyone. The negative words spoken will break you down, destroy any faith in the weak, and keep some captive throughout their lifetimes. The graphics will show three things: (1) what others say about you, (2) your reaction to their words, and (3) your final decision.

I would be remiss not to say what God thinks about you and how you can overcome the negative words spoken over you. Hold on to your faith. Help is coming. Anticipate your deliverance; it is in the last chapter.

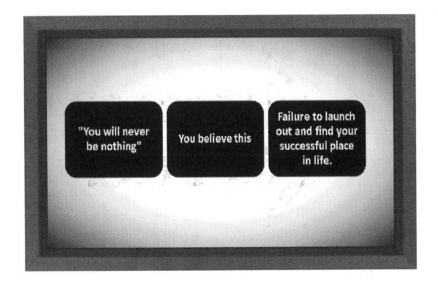

Jesus came into this world to bring you hope.

You can trust in his Word.

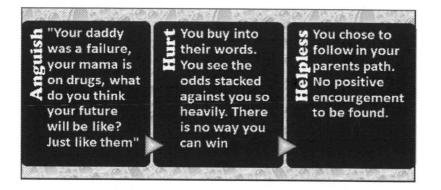

Do not go where evil people go. Do not follow the example of the wicked. Don't do it! Keep away from evil! Refuse it and go on your way. (Proverbs 4:14, 15 GNT)

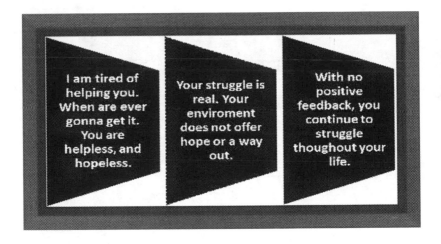

With the new day comes new strength and new thoughts. (Eleanor Roosevelt)[11]

Nobody want you	Failure	Sceptism
You are not attractive, you have bastard children, you are broke. I can't see anybody in their right mind wanting you and your children.	You failed to believe that there is someone out there, looking for a situation like your who want to be your mate, be your provider and be the father of your children.	Gets the best of you and you can not see anything good coming out of your situation. True, you may be lacking financial stability, you are an unwed mother of several and you are not that attractive

Life is like a camera. Just focus on what's important. Capture the good times. Develop from the negative and if things don't turn out, just take another shot.

—Author unknown

The key is to keep company only with people who uplift you, whose presence calls forth your best.

—Epictetus

KILLER Bs

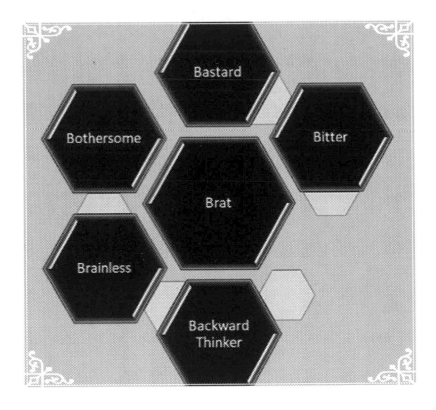

KILLER Bs

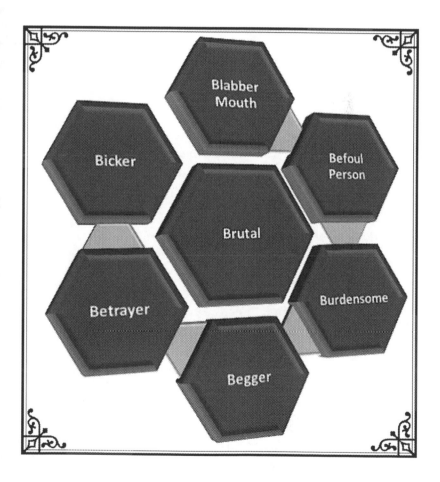

GOD SEES

A POEM BY CHARLOTTE A SPENCER

God sees you as you are. Whenever you cover whether near or far.
He sees the frown behind the closed doors.
You are not hiding because he knows.
Racing thoughts where do I begin to
make all things feel great within.
Trying to think through what you want me to be.
I wait! I wait! I know that you see me.
Everyday I am given a new breath so I
can go on and do my very best.
Each moment when I take a new step, I realize that you see me
and I need your help.
Fear and doubt comes my way. Please
help me to make it another day.
Moaning and tears you know how I feel.
Touch my thoughts and help me to forgive.
God sees the struggle everyday.
Guide me to go a different way.
Anger is seen from time to time. A secret
prayer to relieve my mind.
You have made it easy for me to climb, because
you were watching me all that time.
Whatever you think or dare not say.
I know that God sees me anyway.

HOW DOES GOD SEE ME?

First, I thank the Lord God for endowing me with the gift to capture my thoughts and experiences in a book. I may not be the most excellent speaker or the most celebrated writer, but I use what God has given me and share it in hopes it encourages others.

I had gone back and looked at videos when I ministered in song and was amazed at how God could use someone who once lacked much confidence. It is not about being boisterous but about humbling ourselves before the Lord and allowing Him to shine through us. When I forget about my surroundings and focus on Jesus, everything else fades away. I am comfortable being in my happy place. I begin to see just how much Christ loves and cares for me. I get lost in his presence; there is nothing like it in the world. At times I see this myself, and then at other times, I know what he sees in me. All this happens while I minister in song.

As a youth, the youth president of our local convention suggested that we create a panel of enthusiastic young people to present to the congregation a forum that would test our knowledge of God's Word. The youth president chose me to be on the panel. And as a panelist, I was nervous.

Everyone spoke so confidently and clearly. Lights, camera, and action—now it was time to do something amazing. When it was my turn to speak, I got tongue-tied. The words in my brain were perfect, but when I began to talk, it all came out muttered. I heard one guy on the panel say, "She doesn't know what she is talking about." I suddenly felt like a dwarf. I wanted to go somewhere and hide.

Then just as I was panicking, the Word of the Lord came out of my mouth. It was Ephesians 6:11–17. I quoted them clearly, without missing a beat. The congregation started clapping with much energy, and they gave me a great big, "Amen." I was redeemed! Nonetheless, that was the last panel I participated in as a youth. The Lord has since performed a work in me that I can stand and engage in conversation without fail (calling into existence, those things that be not as though it is).

I could have easily said I would never do that again because of the negative comments. I did not. I channeled my energy in other areas while building up my nerves to go public again.

So what does this story have to do with how God sees us? Only that he was showing me that I can overcome any adversity that arises in my life. God showed me that I was courageous, hanging in until Christ supplied the words. I opened my mouth, and he filled it with his Word. I started confident but faltered along the way. The Lord knew the intent of my heart, and he came through for me.

Over the years, the Spirit of God gave me the mental toughness to boost the areas of my weakness. Sometimes I minister the Word of the Lord to our congregation. Had I not had that experience, I would not have allowed the Lord to complete the great work he started in me. I know that others may be undergoing something similar. All I can say is, "Hang on in there." Christ is not done with you yet.

I heard these old words as a child, and even spoke them myself: "Sticks and stones may break my bones, but words will never hurt." But that well-known phrase is not valid.

Words have power, whether spoken as to be an inspiration or as words to destroy us. As an adult, you may be under constant degrading, but there is hope. You can take your cares to the Lord. He will heal your wounds. As children of the Most High God, we all must be careful of the words we pronounce over our children and even over our enemies. His Word tells us to love our enemies and pray for those who misuse us. Loving and praying for my enemy can be much, especially when the words run deep and are often said. Thus, as we continue to yield ourselves under the mighty hands of God, we experience his unconditional love and faithfulness.

Following is a list of scriptures from the Bible that will help you see just what God thinks and says about you. You can take them to the bank of life and cash it out as pure gold.

- You are the head and not the tail; above only and not beneath (Deuteronomy 28:13 KJV).
- We are his workmanship, created in Christ Jesus unto good works (Ephesians 2:10 KJV).
- We are a chosen generation, a royal priesthood, an holy nation, a peculiar people (1 Peter 2:9 KJV).

- We are not just conquerors; we are more than a conqueror (Romans 8:37 KJV).

- We are a new creature (2 Corinthians 5:17 KJV).

- We can do all things through Christ (Philippians 4:13 KJV).

- We have the same power within us that raised Christ from the dead (Romans 8:11 KJV).

- We are the righteousness of God in Christ Jesus (2 Corinthians 5:21 KJV).

- We are Abraham's seed and heirs according to the promise (Galatians 3:29 KJV).

- We are adopted into the royal family of God (Ephesians 1:5 KJV).

- We will be eating from the tree of life. (Revelation 22:14 KJV).

- We are not ashamed of the gospel of Christ (Romans 1:16 KJV).

- We are fully equipped warriors (Ephesians 6:11–17 KJV).

- We are strong and courageous (Joshua 1:6, 7; Ephesians 6:10 KJV).

- We are willing to sacrifice (Esther KJV).

- We are undying lovers (Hosea KJV).

Outstanding! What a way to end this book—sanctioned by the Word of God. As you stand firm on his promises, Christ will heal those negative wounds; they do not have the rule over you anymore. He gives you the strength to move forward in the name of Jesus, equipped with everything you need to be a success story. I look forward to seeing the champion that you are.

Seeing ourselves through the eyes of God gives us an advantage over the world. It empowers the body of Christ to open our spiritual eyes, walk in faith and confidence, and help us discover just who we are and what we are capable of becoming. May our Lord and Savior continue to be the light to your pathway, the greater one inside of you, and continue to make you good enough until the coming of the Lord.

GLOSSARY

alienated. Experiencing or inducing feelings of isolation or estrangement.

carnal. Pertaining to flesh; fleshly; sensual; opposed to spiritual; as carnal pleasure.

El Elyon. The Most High God. Genesis 14:18–20.

El Shaddai. The All-Sufficient One. The God of the Mountains. God Almighty. He is the all sufficient source of all our blessings. God is all-powerful. Our problems are not too big for God to handle. Genesis 17:1–3.

Elohim. The All-Powerful One, Creator. God is the all-powerful creator of the universe. God knows all, creates all, and is everywhere at all times.

I AM. YHWH. The One Who Is the Self-Existent One. God never changes. He promises never fail. When we are faithless, he is faithful. Exodus 3:14; Malachi 3:6.

Jehovah El-Roi. The God Who Sees Me. There are no circumstances in our lives that escape his fatherly awareness and care. God knows us and our troubles. Genesis 16:11–14.

Jehovah Jireh, The Lord Will Provide. Genesis 22:13–14.

Jehovah-Rohi. The Lord Is My Shepherd. The Lord protects, provides, directs, leads, and cares for his people. God tenderly takes care of us as a strong and patient shepherd. Psalm 23:1–3; Isaiah 53:6.

Jehovah Shalom. The Lord is Peace. Judges 6:24.

Jehovah Tsidkenu. The Lord Our Righteousness. Jesus is the King who would come from David's line and is the one who imparts his righteousness to us. Jeremiah 23:5, 6; Ezekiel 36:26–27.

mustard seed. The small round seeds of various mustard plants. The seeds are usually about 1 to 2 millimeters (0.039 to 0.079 inches) in diameter and maybe colored from yellowish white to black.

Nazarite. An Israelite consecrated to God's service, under vows to abstain from alcohol, let the hair grow, and avoid defilement by contact with corpses. Numbers 6.

repent. To feel or express sincere regret or remorse about one's wrongdoing or sin.

Yahweh-Shemmah. The Lord Is There/Present. Ezekiel 48:35.

NOTES

1   Tracy Robbins, HappyHealthyandProsperous. *Names of God Old Testament*. [Online] 2020. [Cited: July 16, 2020.],https://www.pinterest.com/pin/461126449330904554/

2   FARLEX 2003-2020). "Vision.", The Free Dictionary, s.v. Accessed November 27, 2020, https/www.thefreedictionary.com/visions.

3   Diana Leagh Matthews, "Song Story: Where Could I Go But To The Lord," *Rebel to Redeemed … Sharing His Kind of Love* (blog), February 4, 2018, http://dianaleaghmatthews.com/where-could-i-go-but-to-the-lord/#.Xy72nihKiUl.

4   Joop's Musical Flowers, **"Where Could I Go But to the Lord Lyrics."**, Accessed November 27, 2020; http://jopiepopie.blogspot.com/2014/06/where-could-i-go-1940-where-could-i-go.html

5   Joyce Myers, "Joyce Myers Ministries.org", accessed June 8, 2020; https://joycemeyer.org/shop/Books%3djoycemeyer_usa-books/BattlefieldoftheMind%28LargePrint%29%3d013435

6   History.com Editors, "Spanish Flu," History.com, last modified October 12, 2010; https://www.history.com/topics/world-war-i/1918-flu-pandemic;

7   You Version, "*Ten Plagues of Moses*", Biblegateway.com, chapters 6-12, https://www.bible.com/bible/1/EXO.6.KJV.

8   William Rosen, *Justinian's Flea: Pleague, Empire, and the Birth of Europe* Archived. ID 9, 2007. Accessed July 3, 2020, p.3, http://www.justiniansflea.com/events.htm ; Andrew J. Ekonomou, *Byzantine Roman and the Greek Popes: Eastern Influences on Rome and the Papacy from Gregory the Great to Zacharias, A.D. 590–752.* Accessed July 3, 2020, https://www.google.com/books/edition/Byzantine_Rome_and_the_Greek_Popes/zomZk6DbFTIC?hl=en&gbpv=1; Thomas H. Maugh II, *An Empire's Epidemic: Scientists Use DNA in Search for Answers to 6th Century Plague*, May 6, 2002, Los Angeles Times, https://en.wikipedia.org/wiki/List_of_epidemics.

9   Akihito Suzuki, "Smallpox and the Epidemiological Heritage of Modern Japan: Towards a Total History," Japan: Cambridge Journals Medical History. Accessed July 27, 2020, https://www.ncbi.nlm.nih.gov/pmc/articles/PMC3143877/ ; George C. Kohn, *Encyclopedia of Plague and Pestilence: From Ancient Times to the Present* (Princeton, NJ: Checkmark Books, 2002, p.213), [Cited: July 27, 2020.], https://www.amazon.com/Encyclopedia-Plague-Pestilence-Ancient-Present/dp/0816069352.

10   J. N. Hays, *Epidemics and Pandemics: Their Impacts on Human History. List of epidemics.* [Online] ID 9, 2005. https://en.wikipedia.org/wiki/List_of_epidemics#cite_note-Hays2005p345-148, https://en.wikipedia.org/wiki/List_of_epidemics.

11   Eleanor Roosevelt, "My Day, January 8, 1936," *The Eleanor Roosevelt Papers Digital Edition* (2017), accessed 11/28/2020, https://www2.gwu.edu/~erpapers/myday/displaydoc.cfm?_y=1936&_f=md054227.

ABOUT THE AUTHOR AND ARTIST

Avis D. Brownlee-Wooley, dedicated to the service of the Lord, enjoys writing. She serves in whatever capacity that needs attention. She also serves as minister of music in her local church. *Through God's Eyes* is her second book. The first was *Girls ... God's Best 4 U.* She has written other unpublished materials such as puppetry skits and plays. She has been happily married to Stanley J. Wooley for thirty-nine years. They have three beautiful grandchildren and a boxer named Pierré.

Her passions have, and always will be, caring for the souls of people. She loves to minister to individuals one on one about the saving grace of our Lord and Savior, and his ability to give us the desires of our hearts. Her mission is simple: to fulfill God's plans for her life, and in doing so, bring salvation to the lost, hurting, and dying.

Naomi was born in February 2005 and is the oldest of three children to parents Sasha, Shaun Johnson, and Jay C. Brisker

She is a rising high school student with great aspirations to be a softball player. Some of her hobbies are painting, sketching, photography, music, and being around animals—particularly her boxer, Pierré.

She enjoys helping in her grandparents' ministry, Witness Protection Ministries Inc. Two ways that she contributes to the ministry are singing on the praise team and operating the camera. Naomi has a kind heart. She shows kindness to everyone she meets.

Naomi created the drawing, *Shower with Depression*, to reflect how youth are affected by negative words, ones that tear down and do not build up. Naomi demonstrated a great perception on what was needed when asked to draw an image with only the title told to her.

Naomi, thank you, for using your talent in such a profound way. By the way, Naomi is the granddaughter of the author.

Printed in the United States
By Bookmasters